ZOO ANIMALS IN THE WILD

GIANT PANDA

JINNY JOHNSON

ILLUSTRATED BY GRAHAM ROSEWARNE

W
FRANKLIN WATTS
LONDON • SYDNEY

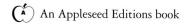 An Appleseed Editions book

First published in 2005 by Franklin Watts
96 Leonard Street, London EC2A 4XD

Franklin Watts Australia
Level 17/207 Kent Street, Sydney, NSW 2000

© 2005 Appleseed Editions

Created by Appleseed Editions Ltd,
Well House, Friars Hill, Guestling, East Sussex TN35 4ET

Designed by Helen James
Illustrated by Graham Rosewarne

ISBN 0 7496 5981 5

A CIP catalogue for this book is available from the British Library

Photographs by China Span (Keren Su), Corbis (Bettmann, Tom Brakefield,
Tim Davis, PARKER HANK/CORBIS SYGMA, Reuters, Keren Su,
VAUGHN BILL/CORBIS SYGMA)

Printed and bound in Thailand

Contents

Giant pandas

With its big, round head, black eye patches, and fluffy ears, the giant panda is one of the most recognizable animals in the world.

Giant pandas look very cute and cuddly. But pandas are a kind of bear, and although they are usually gentle animals, they can be dangerous. They weigh more than most adult people and have strong teeth and claws.

A panda's black and white fur is very thick and woolly.

There are more than 100 giant pandas living in zoos in China, the US, Europe and Japan. Zoo pandas are all born in zoos. They aren't taken from the wild.

A panda's body is plump and chunky, and it has a short tail. Most of a panda's fur is white, but it has black markings on its face, legs and shoulders.

All pandas have black ears and eye rings. But each animal has slightly different markings around its mouth.

At home in the wild

Wild giant pandas live in forests high in the mountains of China, where it is cool, misty and often wet. A panda doesn't have a regular den, but sometimes shelters in a hollow tree or cave.

In the winter, it snows in the mountains where pandas live, and it gets very cold.

A panda grows extra thick fur in winter to keep warm, and loses some fur in summer.

Pandas don't mind the cold because their furry coats keep them warm. Their fur has an oily surface, so water runs off it and the panda stays dry.

No one knows why pandas have black and white fur. Some people think that the bold markings might help pandas find each other in the forests when it's time to mate.

Conifer trees and bamboo plants grow in the panda's mountain home.

At home in the zoo

Giant pandas are some of the most popular of all zoo animals. Zoo pandas need an outdoor area with rocks and trees where they can climb and exercise. Their zoo home must also have an indoor shelter where they can rest, sleep and escape from zoo visitors.

Some of the newest panda enclosures have special rocky areas that are kept cool and damp, like the pandas' home in the wild. Pandas also like to have a pool of water to splash in. When they come out they shake themselves dry.

Snow in the zoo makes it feel like home!

These pandas are having fun on the climbing frame at the National Zoo in Washington, DC.

On the move

Pandas move on all fours most of the time. They usually walk slowly and quietly, but they can move faster and even gallop a short distance. Pandas can also stand up on their back legs for a short time.

Most pandas are good tree climbers. They come down backwards, arm over arm, just as people do.

Every panda moves around its own territory – the area where it finds its food – but doesn't travel very far.

A tree is a comfortable place to sit and rest for a while.

Pandas don't travel very far in the wild, so they don't need a very big home to roam around in the zoo.

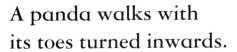

A panda walks with its toes turned inwards.

A panda usually walks about 550 metres a day – about as far as four or five city blocks. The territories of several pandas may overlap, so the animals come across each other once in a while, but they don't spend much time together.

A panda doesn't like to stand upright for too long.

A panda's day

Finding food and eating takes up most of a panda's day. Pandas may be out and about at any time of the day or night, but they are usually busiest around dawn and in the early evening. At least once a day a panda needs to find some water to drink.

Pandas sleep a lot. A panda doesn't make a bed for itself. It just lies down under the nearest tree, and often goes back to favourite spots. A panda sleeps lying on its back or curled up on its side.

A panda laps up fresh water with its tongue.

It sometimes uses its back leg as a pillow or holds one paw over its eyes.

Pandas don't need to spend much time keeping themselves clean. They look after their fur by rolling in dirt or sand to get rid of insects in their fur.

Pandas usually sleep for two to four hours at a time.

A panda enclosure often includes a sandpit where the pandas can roll and clean their fur.

Panda food

Pandas feed on a plant called bamboo. This is a kind of grass that grows in the forests where pandas live. There's not much goodness in bamboo, so the panda has to eat a lot of it – about 12.5 kg a day. That's the same as eating 25 large heads of lettuce!

A panda uses its strong teeth and jaws to crush bamboo into bits.

A panda carefully chooses which pieces of bamboo it wants to eat.

Bamboo is a very tough plant, but the panda has big, broad teeth and very strong jaws for crushing and chewing its food.

Pandas don't eat many other kinds of food, but they will sometimes nibble a few other plants or even catch a small animal such as a mouse.

How a panda eats

A panda has an extra 'thumb' on each front paw to help it hold stems of bamboo in the same way as people hold things. Other bears cannot do this.

The panda sits down on the ground to eat so that its front paws are free to hold the bamboo.

This panda is stripping the leaves from a bamboo stem.

The panda's extra 'thumb' gives it a strong grip.

The panda strips away the tough, outer layer of a bamboo stem with its teeth to reach the softer parts inside. It also picks off the leaves with its fingers and puts them into its mouth.

Zoo pandas eat bamboo too. They're also given small amounts of other treats, such as sugarcane, carrots, apples and sweet potatoes.

Keeping in touch

Wild pandas spend most of their time by themselves, except when they're looking after their young. Pandas are quiet animals, but they make some sounds.

When pandas meet, they may make a bleating call – a bit like a sheep or goat. To scare off an enemy such as a wild dog, a panda may bark or make a chomping sound, bringing its teeth together. A baby panda squeals loudly if it's frightened or is separated from its mother.

A panda scratches a tree trunk as a message to other pandas.

Zoos used to keep pandas by themselves. Now they are finding that young pandas can live happily together and enjoy each other's company.

Pandas also keep in touch by smell. As they wander around the forest, they scratch trees to tell other pandas that they've been there. They may also leave scent messages on trees by spraying a thick liquid from a gland near their tail.

A panda sometimes stands on its hands to leave a scent mark on a tree.

Panda babies

A giant panda gives birth to her cub in
a shelter such as a cave or hollow tree.
Pandas usually have one baby, but
sometimes twins are born.

A newborn panda is tiny —
about the size of a small rat.
It is blind and helpless, with
a scattering of white fur on
its little, pink body.

The mother looks after her baby
by herself. She doesn't leave it at
all for the first two weeks, not
even to eat or drink.

If a mother panda needs to
move her baby, she picks it
up very gently in her mouth.

The mother sits cradling her baby while it feeds on her milk. After each feed, the mother licks her baby to keep it clean.

A newborn panda cub is tiny compared to its mother. She is about 900 times heavier.

When a zoo panda gives birth to twins, the keepers help her take care of the babies. Every day, they switch the babies so that each one has a day with its mother, then a day with the keepers. The keepers bottle-feed the baby pandas.

Growing up

When it's a month old, the panda cub begins to grow black and white fur. Its eyes open a few weeks later. The baby grows quickly. By the time it's three or four months old, it weighs about 5.8 kg – nearly 60 times as much as when it was born.

A panda's milk is rich and fatty, so her cub grows fast.

A panda cub feeds on its mother's milk until it is about nine months old, but it starts to try bamboo when it's five or six months old.

The baby stays close to its mother. If it strays too far, it could be attacked by wild dogs, weasels or stoats. A young panda often scampers up a tree if it's in danger.

Panda cubs have fun chasing each other in the trees.

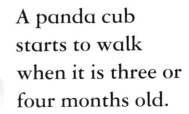

A panda cub starts to walk when it is three or four months old.

23

Playtime

Young pandas love to play. They climb trees – and sometimes fall out of them if they haven't worked out how to climb down. They like tumbling and wrestling with their mother. Even older pandas will roll on the ground and turn somersaults.

This young panda is enjoying playing on his own.

Sometimes pandas also play and splash in water. Playing helps to build up a panda's muscles.

Playing is even more fun with a friend!

Zoo pandas are often more playful than pandas in the wild, and keepers give them toys so they don't get bored. Zoo pandas play with plastic containers, cans, bags or blocks of ice with food treats inside.

Leaving home

By the time it's a year old, a young panda can find all its own food. But it stays with its mother until it is two or three years old. After that, many young pandas stay in territories near their mother, but some young female pandas travel far from home.

A panda is ready to start its own family when it is about five or six years old. Scientists believe that wild pandas can live to be 20 years old.

This young panda is almost as big as his mother. Soon he'll start to live on his own.

Most zoo pandas live longer than wild pandas. The oldest known zoo panda lived to be 34 years old. Researchers study zoo pandas to learn how to help wild pandas survive.

Grown-up pandas usually stay well away from each other, but this mother and son seem very happy chewing bamboo together.

Panda fact file

Here is some more information about giant pandas. Your mum or dad might like to read this, or you could read these pages together.

The giant panda is a mammal. It belongs to the bear family. People used to think that giant pandas belonged to the raccoon family. The lesser panda, also called the red panda, is part of the raccoon family and looks much more like a raccoon than a bear.

Where giant pandas live

Wild giant pandas live only in bamboo forests in the mountains of southwest China.

Panda numbers

Giant pandas are now very rare. Scientists think that there are only about 1,600 living in the wild. Large areas of the forests where they live have been cut down, and many pandas were captured and killed by poachers in the past. Now, pandas and the areas where they live are very strictly protected, but some pandas are still killed by poachers.

Size

The giant panda is about 1.2–1.5 metres long, with a short tail about 12 cm long. It weighs 75–160 kg. A newborn baby panda weighs only 100 g, but by the time it's about three months old, it can weigh up to 5.8 kg.

Find out more

World Wildlife Fund: Pandas
http://www.worldwildlife.org/pandas

Smithsonian National Zoological Park: Giant Pandas
http://www.nationalzoo.si.edu/Animals/giantpandas

San Diego Zoo: Giant Panda
http://www.sandiegozoo.org/animalbytes/t-giant_panda.html

ARKive Images of Life on Earth
http://www.arkive.org/species/GES/mammals/Ailuropoda_melanoleuca

Words to remember

cub
A young animal such as a bear or panda.

enclosure
The area where an animal lives
in the zoo.

gland
A part of the body that makes
a special substance, such as the
liquid pandas use to leave scent
messages.

gallop
A fast movement made
by a four-legged animal.

mammal

A warm-blooded animal, usually with four legs and some hair on its body. Female mammals feed their babies with milk from their own body.

mate

To produce babies.

poacher

Someone who hunts an animal without permission.

territory

The area where an animal spends most of its time and finds its food.

Index